WHAT IN SAM HILL?

ISBN 0-88336-280-5

New Readers Press
Publishing Division of Laubach Literacy International
Syracuse, New York

KALEIDOSCOPE
A Collection of Stories

WHAT IN SAM HILL?

by Sara Hoskinson Frommer

New Readers Press • Syracuse, New York

ISBN 0-88336-280-5

© 1991 Sara Hoskinson Frommer

Published by
New Readers Press
Publishing Division of
Laubach Literacy International
Box 131, Syracuse, New York 13210

All rights reserved. No part of this book may be reproduced or transmitted in any form or by any means, electronic or mechanical, including photocopying, recording, or by any information storage and retrieval system, without permission in writing from the publisher.

Printed in the United States of America

Series Editor: Teddy Norwich Kempster
Editor: Maria A. Collis
Illustrations: Anne Bialke
Cover design: Patti DiCarlo
Cover illustration: Gerald Russell

9 8 7 6 5 4 3 2 1

Contents

1. Sam Goes Shopping............ 5
2. Sam Shops for Jenny........... 11
3. Sam Eats Ribs 15
4. Jenny Comes to Supper........ 18

1. Sam Goes Shopping

Sam Hill hates shopping. But Sam lives alone. He's a good cook, and he likes to eat. So he goes to the supermarket.

Sam has lived alone a long time. He's shopping for a wife, too.

They say the supermarket is a good place to meet women. But Sam never meets women there.

Today, Sam sees a woman with a child.

"I want a cookie," the child says. "Daddy gives me a cookie."

"We'll take some cookies home to Daddy," says the woman.

"She's taken," Sam thinks. He takes a shopping cart.

He looks at his shopping list. He forgets to look where he's going. By the fancy foods, Sam's cart hits a woman. She falls down.

"What in Sam Hill!" she yells.

"I'm sorry!" says Sam Hill. "I didn't see you. Are you OK?"

He looks down at her. She feels her arms and legs.

"I think so," she says. She sticks out her hand. Taking her hand, Sam helps her up.

She is little. Sam likes that. He's not a tall man. He likes her face, too.

What a way to meet a woman!

"I'm glad you're OK," Sam says. He's still holding her hand. "I'm Sam Hill."

"You're not!" She laughs. "You're making that up!"

She's pretty when she laughs. Maybe the supermarket IS a good place to meet women. Sam lets go of her hand.

"I'm stuck with my name," Sam says. "But it's not all bad. It made you laugh."

"Yes, it did," she says. "Hello, Sam Hill. I'm Jenny Sims."

They stand there. Sam sucks in his gut. He wants to look good to Jenny.

"Do you come here a lot?" he says.

"All the time," she says. "I have to eat. And they say it's a good place to meet men. But I never met a man I liked before."

"Before!" Sam thinks. "She said 'before!' She likes me!"

Jenny smiles at Sam. Then she puts some rice in her shopping cart. It's fancy wild rice.

"She likes fancy food," thinks Sam. He looks at the fancy foods. He puts a can of clams in his cart. Fancy smoked baby clams. "Now she'll think I like fancy food, too," he thinks.

"I'll see you," Jenny says. But Sam thinks he won't see her. Not after today. And he wants to.

"Don't go yet," he says. "I'm sorry I ran you down. Can't I make it up to you? Take you to supper?"

"Thanks," Jenny says. "But I like to eat at home."

"You do? Me, too!" says Sam. "I'm a good cook. Let me cook supper for you. I'll feel better."

Jenny smiles up at him.

Sam feels tall.

"OK," Jenny says. "I'll come. I like good cooking."

Sam tells her where he lives. They set a time. Then Jenny goes off.

2. Sam Shops for Jenny

Now Sam is shopping for Jenny. Now it's more fun. But it's harder.

"She likes fancy food," he thinks. "What can I fix?"

He looks at the fancy foods.

Wild rice. He can cook that, and Jenny will like it. He saw her put wild rice in her shopping cart.

Sam puts wild rice in his cart.

Pine nuts. "I'll mix pine nuts with the wild rice," he thinks. He puts pine nuts in his cart.

Baby corn. He sees little ears of corn in jars. He puts two little jars in his cart.

And cheese. But what kind of cheese? Cheddar cheese? Extra sharp cheddar? Black wax cheddar? Swiss cheese? Baby Swiss?

"That's it," Sam thinks. "Baby Swiss cheese. To go with the baby corn and the baby clams." He puts the baby Swiss cheese in his cart.

Kumquats. "What's a kumquat?" Sam thinks. "One way to find out." He takes a jar of kumquats.

Sauce. Mint sauce. Pepper sauce. Hard sauce.

Sam likes to make sauce. He doesn't need sauce from the supermarket.

Sam likes white bread. But for Jenny, he gets dark bread.

He still needs meat. Sam loves ribs. Ribs are what he cooks best. He makes good sauce for them. He eats them with beans and hot sauerkraut.

"I can't fix ribs and sauerkraut for Jenny," Sam thinks. "That's not fancy food. Ribs are down-home food."

Sam puts some ribs in his cart. The ribs are for him. He puts in a duck for Jenny. "Duck with wild rice," he thinks. "Now that's fancy."

3. Sam Eats Ribs

The next day, Sam fixes the ribs. He puts his good sauce on them.

Sam likes his ribs tender. He cooks them a long time. All day he puts sauce on them. All day he smells them. Mmmm.

Then he heats some beans. Sam makes his sauce, but his beans come from a can.

He heats some sauerkraut. The sauerkraut comes from a can, too.

At last the ribs are tender. The meat is falling off the bones. Sam eats ribs with his fingers. He mops up the sauce with white bread.

It's a wonderful supper.

"Poor Jenny," Sam thinks. "Look what she's missing. But duck will be good."

4. Jenny Comes to Supper

The doorbell rings.

Sam wipes his face. He wipes his fingers, too. Ribs are good, but they're messy.

Then Sam goes to the door. It's Jenny.

"Jenny!" Sam just stands there. He thinks, "What's she doing here today?"

"Hi, Sam," Jenny says. "Aren't you going to let me in?"

"Sorry," Sam says. "Come on in." He steps back.

"Mmmm, it smells wonderful!" Jenny says. She takes her coat off. She gives it to Sam.

He stands there with Jenny's coat. He looks at her pretty dress. Jenny's all dressed up.

Sam looks at his pants. He looks at his shirt. He's a mess.

"Well?" says Jenny.

"Well, what?" Sam thinks. Then he thinks, "Oh, no! Jenny thinks the supper she smells is for her. How did this happen?"

Jenny looks at Sam's face. She looks at his messy pants and shirt.

"Oh, no, Sam!" she says. "Did I mix up the date?"

"That's OK," he says. But he keeps his back to the table. He doesn't want Jenny to see what he's eating.

Jenny does see.

"Ribs!" she says. "Sam, I just love ribs!"

"You do?" says Sam. "You do?"

"Let me stay," she says. "Let me eat ribs with you."

Sam lays Jenny's coat down.

"Please stay," he says. "I have lots of ribs. I have beans and sauerkraut, too. But Jenny, you put wild rice in your cart. Don't you like fancy food? I got lots of fancy food for you."

"No," says Jenny. "I like down-home food. Don't you like fancy food? We met by the fancy foods. You put baby clams in your cart. I don't like clams!"

"Then why did you come?" says Sam.

"Not for the clams!" Jenny laughs. "I came for you, Sam Hill. I like you. And now I get ribs, too. This is wonderful!"

Sam gives her a little hug. "You're wonderful, Jenny," he says.

And, wonder of wonders, she hugs him back. She does like him!

Sam takes Jenny to the table. He gives her a big plate of ribs. "Eat all you want, Jenny. Lots more where these came from."

Jenny eats ribs with her fingers, too. She mops up the sauce with white bread.

Sam sits and looks at her.

"Jenny," he says.

"Yes, Sam?"

"What are we going to do with all that fancy food?"